One year of Poetry
2020 - 2021

A Poetry Anthology
Edited by
Lis McDermott

The Authors assert the moral right to be identified as the owners of the work. All poems are entirely the work of the author's imagination. Any resemblance to actual persons, living or dead, events or localities is entirely coincidental.
All rights are reserved.

No part of this publication may be used, reproduced, stored in a retrieval system or transmitted, in any form or by any means, electronic, mechanical, photocopying, recording, or otherwise, without prior permission from the publishers.

This book is sold subject to the condition that it shall not, by the way of trade or otherwise, be lent, re-sold, hired out or otherwise circulated without the publisher's prior consent in any form of binding or cover, other than that, in which it is published and without a similar condition including this condition being imposed on the subsequent purchaser

Copyright Compilation: ©Lis McDermott 2021
Copyright Poems: ©Individual Named Authors 2021
Copyright Cover: ©Lis McDermott

Publisher: Pen & Ink Designs 2021

ISBN: 9781915086044

LIS' POETRY PLACE

Lis' Poetry Place is an online group of poets who have met during the last two years. Some members have come and gone, but these are the core members for this year.

Led by Lis McDermott, we meet monthly to share the poems written during the month by group members; share poems by other poets, introducing the group to poets perhaps previously unheard, and we explore different poetry forms.

Group members are all at different stages in their poetry journey. For more information please see the information at the end of the book.

CONTENTS

Each section is made up of a group of poems written for specific prompts set throughout the year.

Individual poets responded in their own styles, to the prompts reacting to their personal feelings about the subject matter.

Poets Bios can be found on page 233.

Inspired by Book Titles.

HINDSIGHT

It frightens me to think
I spent years
Believing in our shared story.
That I gave myself the title of Co-Author
When in reality,
It was just me writing, re-writing
The history
I wanted to recount.

It frightens me to think
I tried to straighten up my round edges.
Planted the idea of us in the ground
And prayed for you to grow into
The version I wanted you to be.
That I made peace with the worst,
Made-believe it was my destiny.

It frightens me to know
There never was a Place for Us.
For you and me,
Together.
Equally.

Greeshma Rajeev

Inspiration: "A Place for Us" -Fatima Mirza

Before the black shadows meet the light,
They lurk.
Silently grim,
Their eyes glistening midst pallid faces.
No ageing crones,
But youthful creatures,
Expectant lips salivating,
Waiting for the hour,
When shadows dissipate.
Their eyes sharpen upon sight
Of any soul caught venturing out
At the wrongful hour of night.
Anticipation of the time,
When the glare of the sun is replaced
By the shade of the killing moon,
Only then can the carnage begin.
The atmosphere becoming thick
With the stench of blood, viscera and death,
As would-be innocents, forever young,
Change into monsters of the night,
And for the first and last time,
Their prey, even grown men
Fall victim to the occult,
The Midnight's Children.

Lis McDermott

Inspiration: "Midnight's children" Salman Rushdie

VIRGIN EARTH

Dappled rays of sun light dancing, beaming
patterns through primeval trees.
Illuminating, warming, sparkling, caressing;
life is awakening on the forest floor.
Insects scurrying, animals burrowing; green
shoots pushing up through fertile earth.
Seeds germinating, berries ripening as the
morning temperature soars.

Animals roaming free and easy, watchfully
grazing on a sea of rich tall grass.
Hunters hunting low and insistent, skilfully
stalking their evening repast.
The heavens awake with flocks of birds of
many colours soaring high into the sky.
Synchronised, swooping, climbing, flaunting
a spectacular feathered display.

Alien trees, plants and shrubs grow in
profusion, a kaleidoscope of colours, a
collectors dream,
A fast river thunders on, flowing over rocks and
boulders, into turbulent rapids,
cascading over waterfalls, running on to reach the
sea.

Wild trout and salmon swim upstream leaping through the spray,
Rocky cliffs and promontories rise up majestically on either side.

Do not be deceived by this beautiful Eden, the wilderness inhospitable as such,
even natives battle to survive.
A virgin world, where man is a stranger, has not left his mark;
Beautiful plants and shrubs thrive,
Animals and birds free to live naturally.

>   Carolyne Crawford

Inspiration: "Virgin Earth" - Phyllippa Gregory

So extraneous are my tears
that I often wonder
if the master, resting
in His alcazar
beyond blue yonder,
ever bothers.

Too busy running the cosmos,
does he pay heed to
my aching heart
and how it's torn apart?
my missing smile
all this while,
endless pitfalls
that leave me appalled?
and this gift of life, with
melancholy running rife?

Hadn't He been so careless,
a reckless self-indulgent king,
He would have assigned mini-Gods
to mind such small things.

Naman Kumar

Inspiration: "God of Small Things" Arundhati Roy

Just Because

JUST BECAUSE

I didn't stop smiling, just because the sun didn't shine
I didn't cry, just because you weren't there
I didn't stop breathing, just because the sky grew dark
I didn't give up reading, just because the libraries closed
I didn't stop being me, just because I grew older
No – I did none of these, and I never will.
Why? Just because.

Ann Brady

THE NEXT RELATIONSHIP

Just because it wasn't you
Who gave me a swollen lip that first time,
Does not mean I won't flinch and fumble
Every time you raise your voice
Just a few decibels higher than you should

Just because you tell me you're different
Or chide me for believing you ever could
Doesn't mean my body will comply
My being is now a frantic, paranoid, wise ol' turtle
It will remember, retreat, make sure I'm alive

And just because I haven't given up on love,
Doesn't mean my body doesn't know how to survive.

Greeshma Rajeev

Just because they turn
blind eye to your fire,
just because they find
it so hard to admire,
just because of the seed
of doubt they sow,
just because their trust
is dreadfully low,
just because it needs
persistence to grow,
just because you've suffered
more than a blow,
just because the Sun doesn't
enlighten your today,
just because you're snowed
under a pile of dismay,
just because it's facile
to accept the defeat,
just because you're born to win,
keep striving on repeat.

                        Naman Kumar

Just because ……

When the sun forgets to shine school holidays can be a terrible bore;
Children cooped up indoors becomes a horrible chore.
Just because it's raining cats and dogs, the sky is dark and grey, there's no need for dismay.
Don their wellies and macs, let them go outside to brave the bad weather today.
Very soon their friends will come along to play;
Then just because it's tremendous fun, with a mighty run, they can dive headlong, into the glorious, muddy puddles with a splish, splash, splosh.
Don't write the whole day off, just because it's miserable and wet;
You never know, today may turn out to be one of the best times yet.

       Carolyne Crawford

Just because the sunniest sky is blue,
Just because I only ever wanted to dance with you
Just because the stars in the night sky glowed brighter
Just because when you made me laugh, I felt lighter.
Just because trees lose their leaves in the fall
Just because you stopped answering my call.
Just because you were kissing another girl
Just because my whole life started to unfurl.
Just because all the oceans of the world lost their tides
Just because friends told you I'd run away to hide.
Just because when you left to live with her last May
Just because no one even noticed, I'd faded away….

                                          Lis McDermott

Slavery

IMAGINE

Imagine knowing your ancestors were
Treated as chattel, considered as property
To be bought and sold,
With little chance of you living to be old.

Imagine having no control of your life,
Being given as a birthday gift
To a child; answering to their every whim,
When you may be not much older than him.

Imagine a female slave, giving birth;
Your child when born, taking its first breath
Will automatically become enslaved,
Even their children's children, and onwards to the grave.

Imagine when captured and torn
From your family and loved ones,
Stripped of your uniqueness, your name,
Henceforth known by your owners' surname.

Imagine the feeling, hundreds of years on
Centuries after the abolition of slavery,
Unaware of your ancestor's place of birth,
Reliable records, a complete dearth.

Imagine living with the loss of family identity,
Your name inherited from a slave owner, to boot;
A continuing insult with which to contend,
For some, never easy to comprehend.

       Lis McDermott

SLAVERY CONDITIONS IN THE MILLS

Imposing factories arose with belching
chimneys and cooling towers.
The production of cotton cloth became
Britain's new heritage.
Slave labour in America provided raw cotton
for industrial change and growth.

Life in the mill was neither healthy nor
pleasant.
Tragically workers, though not slaves, were
treated as such.
The poor, abandoned country life, enticed by
promises of housing, new life and steady pay.
Dreams were cruelly shattered, housing
became filthy, stinking, disease ridden slums.

Health and Safety did not exist, accidents were
common, limbs and lives were easily lost.
Men, women and children worked tortuous,
gruelling hours for very little pay.
The only respite being one- or two-weeks
unpaid holiday a year.

The noise of the machines was deafening,
causing many to lose hearing.
The air was thick with cotton dust, it was
humid and hot.
Many illnesses left workers fighting for breath.
Harsh conditions provoked strikes, soon
workers demanded reform.
In desperation, the first trade union was born.

                              Carolyne Crawford

HEGEMONY

The goal cannot be constant oppression
For it is too hard to whip, trod, and detain.
A quick letdown of the guard
And you might see free legs running across your terrain.

The goal, then, has to be the re-learning of worth
Where you engrave their inferiority
Into the folds of their skin, the beat of their hearts
Until it's all that they can see.

The short-term vision might have been the economy,
But the real endgame is unaffected by time.
Even if a well-meaning *superior* were to offer to hold the ladder,
The response would be a simple thank you,
But I don't dare climb.

Greeshma Rajeev

Hegemony – consent to the rule of the dominant group (as I 'Cultural Hegemony' by Antonio Gramsci)

What they abolished was the slavery
See-able by naked eyes;
what remains is the slavery,
indiscernible - it thrives.

In contempt of nature's laws,
the Whites decided to oppress;
leaving the Africans following commands,
nonplussed, in fear and distress.

Civilizations, since the beginning, have
lacked acumen the most.
Driven by dark, boorish traits,
about fake strength, they boast.

The wheel of fate turns;
it turned for one and all.
Fair sense prevailed;
Human bondage, to an extent, stalled.

Dozing serpent of servitude,
again, rose its hood.
Who'll turn into deadly mongoose, to
put it to sleep for good?

                    Naman Kumar

Unlocked

Her ear-to-ear affirming smile
unlocked a can of gleeful flies;
they flew across miles and miles
spreading infectious bliss with reprise.

Birds met them and chirped euphony,
flowers, by their mere touch, bloomed.
Clouds vacillated with joy and drizzled,
hills and valleys got perfumed.

Tides rose high without a full moon,
peacocks strutted with their feather train.
The Sun shone brighter and stars glazed
to pump up the cosmos with energy insane.

At a loss for words with a pounding heart,
wondering how bits of my fate flocked,
I crave for our love to last eternity
and wish for the 'can' to stay unlocked.

                              Naman Kumar

LIFE UNLOCKING

Life is unlocking, coming alive;
Stretching, awakening from a dark, evil
dream.
Will I feel joy or fear, when I venture into a
changed, chaotic world today?
Am I an intrepid explorer, fearless and bold, or
prisoner, in my own home?
I've read endlessly media reports, revealing
counts of the dead.
They whirl and swirl inside my head.
I'm filled with fear and terrible dread.
Today is my "D Day", as Winston once said.
I won't surrender to doom and gloom.
FaceTime and Zoom aren't consistent with
meeting people face to face.
I mourn the absence of family and friends.
Life is for living not hiding away.
It feels emotional and good, the first time out in
the wide world, after months and months.

                        Carolyne Crawford

OWN PERSON

Recently, thanks to time or luck,
I unlocked a part of me
That I can no longer stash away.

A tiny cocoon, a flash of brilliance.
Light as spirit but with one hell of a fight within it.
The revolution inside the wall of my own skin,
Won't let me quit.

I can no longer,
Pretend I don't deserve it
Believe I can't achieve it
Feel hopeless, dejected,
Un-responsible.
I can no longer
Accept the impossible.

But there are times when all this self-belief
Causes me a lot of fatigue,
So, I try to sneak in while she's going to bed.
Whisper all the reasons she is doomed to fail.
Tie her down, pull her back
Wrap her into the shadows again.

But this feeling, this confidence
It's much too strong for me, I'm afraid.
She's her own person now
And ever since I've unlocked her
She won't let me hide away.

                      Greeshma Rajeev

Acrostic Poems
Colours

Turquoise colours of greens and blue,
Undulating waves, rise and swell
Resplendent in watery majesty
Quintessentially, heaven sent;
Underwater, turquoise star fish, cling to
Oceans reefs, beneath
Incandescent swathes of water, coloured
deepest blue,
Sparkling, sunlit, creating tranquillity and
Endlessly calming my soul.

      Lis McDermott

Suffused with charming myriad hues,
Autumn arrives, shaking off the summer heat.
Laden with picturesque trees that
Morning mists try best to hide,
Only to give in to the September sun,
New season blesses us with crisp vibes.

Part and parcel once, pariah now,
Irrespective, the falling leaves hold their glow.
Nature imparts the wisdom of how
Kingly and pretty is the art of letting go.

                        Naman Kumar

Wild, desolate, pine clad forests, growing on rugged mountain-slopes, covered in virgin, white fluffy snow.
Hear distant rumblings of avalanches floating through
the air, warning of snow slides; skiers and hikers beware.
Icy, beautifully intricate patterns on windowpanes, allegedly created by elusive Jack Frost.
Thoughts of drinking delicious chocolate, creamy and
hot, lifting spirits, warming freezing bodies and hands.
Edelweiss, stunning swathes of pure white daisies, flowering on alpine mountaintops.

                    Carolyne Crawford

Back when I was a little girl, sneaking into my
grandfather's teakwood rocking chair, with my teddy
bear and chocolate bar,
brown was the color of comfort.

Rarely did I spend time thinking about the
one thing news channels can't seem to stop
discussing now.
The color of my skin and what it means.

Over the years, I have marveled at fake-tans that
don't quite
seem right, at hazelnut colored contact lenses, at
coffee - tinted moisturizers,
at wooden décor ideas and chocolate fudge delights.

We crave the color brown, but then why
does my skin feel unwanted in a sea of light,
an intruder, an immigrant, a thief in the night?

Now, more than ever, I see my brothers and sisters
struggle for acceptance and long to belong,
and I am convinced that peace and equality are the
color brown.

Greeshma Rajeev

Autumn

AUTUMN

Don't be melancholy at summer's end;
Observe nature's beauty preparing for winter chills.
Decreased sunlight heralds a season of swirling mists, crisp frosty mornings, storms, shorter days, longer nights.
First batches of leaves falling from trees.
Spectacular landscapes transformed into colourful hues;
Vivid yellows, oranges, flaming reds.
Squirrels hiding nuts for later feasts.
Pungent wood smoke from roaring bonfires wafting through the air.
Reminisce halcyon days of childhood, playing conkers, kicking leaves underfoot.
Harvests of lush abundance; rose hips, sloe gin, elderberry wine, blackberry and apple pie.
Great time to breakout jackets, coats, boots, scarves and hats.
Perfect setting for the senses; comfort, warmth, reflection.

Carolyne Crawford

Autumn comes with colours of red and gold
Untold beauty we are told
Trees they shake their golden leaves around
Uttering and swaying in the breeze
Memories of the summer past
Now Autumn is finally here at last

                    Ann Brady

Autumn arrives whilst summertime grieves
Hoarding squirrels run, like little thieves
they ferry nuts in their cheeks to bury,
Darting out in the crisp autumn leaves.

Breezy winds announce cooler weather,
Morning frost covers mountain heather,
Low lying mist hides tree-tops in the copse.
They lean-in, growing close together.

Hearty meals ready, to keep out cold,
Sat at firesides, scary tales are told,
Monsters are carved, pumpkins flayed of their skin,
A Halloween welcome to behold.

Prepare for the Autumn chilly blues
with the luscious golds and russet hues.
A Harvest moon above a forest strewn
with autumn colours, for you to choose.

                        Lis McDermott

Instruction poems

INSTRUCTIONS TO MY UNBORN CHILD

From the moment that sunlight
creeps in to caress your eyes,
know in your fragile bones
that I love you.

When a grown-up tells you
that you have a talent for something,
smile and accept,
but also remember
that talent is the superstar,
hard work is the crew.
Without the crew, the star is
just another person
who can't get the mic to work.

In times of great despair,
look intently at your hands,
which might be mine or your father's,
or those of your ancestors.
Trace the outline with a finger,
let it linger in the valleys and peaks,
those uneven mountain ridges
that you carry around without breaking a sweat.
Life will be okay if you let it.

Know that if you try your hardest,
it will happen. It might take a while -

years that you feel you do not have –
except time isn't measured in years,
it's measured in smiles and laughs,
the arches of our backs.
Learn to channel your inner Monarch butterfly.
Do not despair, do not sigh or roll your eyes,
learn to spread your wings and fly,
knowing in the depths of your stomach -
that inside you, there is a sea
and right now, this is exactly
where you need to be.

If you are anything like your mother,
you will think and think
until your thoughts swirl around
with a life of their own –
broken pieces of wood and plastic
swept up in a tornado
of anxiety and sighs.
They will tell you it won't be alright,
trust me, all lies.

On those lonely nights,
reach for the phone, you are not alone.
From the moment that sunlight
creeps in to caress your eyes,
know in your fragile bones
that I love you.

        Greeshma Rajeev

THE PERFECT GRANDMA MANUAL

First impressions are important;
Grandma greets with sparkling, happy smiles;
Always loving, encouraging, gentle, kind;
Offers cuddles, hugs, kisses;
Is thoughtful, doesn't hurt, or speak her mind;
Forgives, forgets silly, naughty pranks;
Displays the patience of a saint;
Never shouts, becomes frustrated, angry or mad,
or threatens to unleash the wrath of Mum and Dad;
Is a diplomat, mediator of arguments and fights;
Qualified First Aider, treats bruises, bumps and bites;
Keeper of pretty boxes of sticky sweets and
treats, hidden out of reach;
Gives generously at Christmas, birthdays, holidays;
A loyal friend, when times are tough;
Staunch protector when life is rough;
Requires a second set of eyes, ideally situated at the
rear of her head;
Additionally, a sixth sense that can determine a lie
before it's said;

A cordon-bleu cook, creator of delicious dinners all grandkids love;
Enjoys a well-earned G & T after an exhausting day;
Must be an angel, sent from Heaven above.

        Carolyne Crawford

HOW TO SELL A HUSBAND

First make sure he looks as best he can,
So, he outshines every other man
in the online second-hand husband shop,
Which is where I'm uploading him. Next stop.

Step two; write out the advert hoping to entice
a sale, reaching the bidding price.
He is past his sell by date,
and his bedroom performance, dull of late.
Cooking is not his style, but he can definitely clean
though not like Freddy Mercury, in the video by Queen.
He has let his body go, and his belly hangs too low,
which is just fine, if you fancy squidging a tummy of dough!

Step three: take a photograph of his best side,
Let people see, he has nothing to hide.
Get a good close-up of his smiling eyes,
That is what I would advise.

Step four: Decide on costing; important as the seller
After all, for years, as husbands go, he's been a great fella'.

Step five: Set the terms and conditions,
because, this one of my most important missions.
Once seen, you cannot return him, he is not on approval,
although you can get first refusal,
There is no way you can buy one get one free,
because try as you might, make a plea - there is only one of he.

Step six: Finalise any discounts and offers,
I do want a decent amount for him to add to the coffers!
I can offer you a deal today if he is the man you seek,
So, hurry, the offer only lasts for this week.

                                      Lis McDermott

WALKING

With care you stand, and slightly wobble
You hold your breath in case you topple.

Leaning hard upon the sticks, your heart pounds out loud.
Your back you straighten, hoping your leg stands proud.

Then moving with care, you lift your foot
Placing it down slowly, without taking a look.

A sigh of relief you let explode
As the second foot, you slowly unfold.

You place it down gently upon the floor
Shout hooray as that's two steps towards the door.

And so, you try it all again, one foot at a time as if in a dance.
And even tho' you slowly go, you feel as if you've moved as if at a prance.

Ann Brady

Halloween

FRANKENSTEIN

Mothers eyes,
Dads mouth,
Grandmother's hair,
Grandad's nose,
Uncles build,
Auntie's temperament;
We are all made from
The hearts of ancestors;
Like Frankenstein's monster,
A sum of many parts.

Lis McDermott

HALLOWEEN HAIKU

Black cats, giant bats,
things that go bump in the night;
Tonight's Halloween.

Ghosts haunt all the streets;
Tightly wrapped up in white sheets,
giggling in delight.

Skeletons, monsters,
Costumed gaily dressed creatures,
prowling all about.

Dark, black, moonless skies
Loud thunder and lightning strikes
Terrors of the night.

                Carolyne Crawford

SAMHAIN (SOW-WIN)
AN ANCIENT HALLOWEEN

The summer's ended, the harvest gathered in
The Celtic Samhain festival is about to begin.
As the lightness of summer passes and disappears
The dark half of the year is waiting at the rear
It's during Samhain those otherworldly denizens gather near
The Celts have always celebrated their coming at this time of year.
Wearing gaudy costumes and masks to allay their great fear
They hope it will protect them against the deathly smiles of the spirits drawing near
Sacred bonfires they will burn throughout the night
Crops and animal skins will be sacrificed
The aim is to appease the spirits of the under-world
And also, to see if fortunes and marriages are to be foretold
Yet, now these days, we light up the sky
With fireworks which go bang, which flash and fly
And even though we burn a guy

Halloween is held to really help us try
To keep those otherworldly spirits from the door
To prevent us getting bad luck, or maybe more.
Regardless of how, or why you celebrate Halloween
Remember the Celts too once had spirits to wean.

        Ann Brady

If Death was a Choice

IF DEATH WAS A CHOICE

Gift a playful monkey
a hollow glass-ball,
witness how he gets
ecstatic and enthralled.

But your thumping heart knows
at any fateful moment,
you may find it slithered -
badly, brutally broken.

As iffy and capricious
as a monkey I am,
with numerous mindless choices
causing self-inflicted pain.

Novice in comprehending
intricacies of life,
I fear I'd throw it away
if death was a choice.

Oblivious of the beauty, and
worth of my existence,
I'd let the adept master
guard this boon from my nuisance.

                Naman Kumar

IF DEATH WAS A CHOICE ....

Born out of love;
live well to survive.
Patiently following nature's path,
progressively unto death.

Live in the joyous light of life,
or sorrowful darkness
of untimely death.
The choice is ultimately Thine.

Carolyne Crawford

I could not face having to leave this mortal coil,
Not while I'm still enjoying my life, my creative juices still on the boil…
The idea of missing out on what tomorrow might bring,
Opportunities, people, places – all things which make my days 'zing'.
Living without these choices, is beyond my comprehension,
and would be like living in another dimension.
I may feel differently if faced with an incurable disease,
Then death might be something I'd willingly seize.
Maybe when I'm far older than now,
There will come a time when I'll take a bow,
Graciously accept I don't have immortality,
Look forward to hell's hospitality!

                            Lis McDermott

Unspoken Thoughts

BEING HUMANS

Once upon a time,
a pandemic decided to test the theory
that our eyes are the windows to our souls,
by making us cover all the other parts up
so that now, we'd have to
smile with our eyes,
scowl with our brows,
express gratitude with a blink,
and see everything a little more clearly,
than we used to.

Look at us go, tiny masked humans
in barely packed trains and on seldom-occupied sidewalks,
peering into the windows of the other's souls
to see if they're smiling at us.

Look at us beat the first wave and the second,
they're no match for our determinations
to see the ones we love,
to drink a drink and eat a meal,
to brave a pandemic in search for an
unmasked look of happiness that says
It is *so* good to see you.

Look at us sink into our couches,
as the realization sinks into our hearts,
that it will be a long time before things go back, to
Normal.

Look at us brew cups of tea and sit down with each other to
reminisce dinner parties and underground raves,
crowded speakeasys and football stadiums,
and every now and then, look at us scrambling through the grey,
to find a silver lining.
Look at us being human in the face of everything
that pulls us apart.

Greeshma Rajeev

ENOUGH IS ENOUGH

There comes a time to say enough
When family lets you down.
When friends forget to call your name
And life seems coloured, only brown.

You've done your best throughout the years
To help and encourage them all
But suddenly, for some stupid reason
They cannot be bothered now to call

And when they do, it's not quite right
Because they really don't want you
No, just your money, your cash, your loot
Otherwise they end up feeling blue

You know that they don't really care
Whether you smile, or whether you cry.
Perhaps sometime they'll change their minds
Rethinking it all on the day you die.

For that's the day when the Will is read
As they sit and rub their hands with glee
'Tough shit,' it'll say, 'ha ha to you,
I've already had a big spending spree!'

The money, it is all now gone
I spent it here and there
You see you didn't want just me
But only my money to share.

And in that moment maybe they'll think
How kinder they could have been
It's far too late. As I say, "enough is enough.
Your chances are no longer to be seen."

                    Ann Brady

CONVERSATIONS ON A BUS

Sitting on the bus, listening to every conversation,
You hear everything under creation!
Of course, you can't say a thing,
Just decide, which voices to hear sling
information about their family and friends,
Sharing all sorts of odds and ends.
I don't mean to be judgemental,
But some people, look like they belong in a mental
Institution… though I'm one to talk,
I certainly don't have the final solution!
If I thought about what they're saying about me,
I'd be the first to get off and walk!
The guy sitting across from me has begun to snore.
 I wonder if he knows he has the odour
of last night's garlic bread clinging to his every pore?
Snippets of conversations heard,
My mind flits like a flighty, little bird…
That fat girl, should not be wearing that outfit,
At her size, she could block the suns orbit!
I notice a new passenger, a young guy,
Who seems to be quite shy.
Mmm, he looks good, though; in fact, quite hot,
I wonder if he's married.? No ring. He's not!

Behind me things that should be kept unsaid,
Float to my ears; this is how rumours spread.
"Shirl, last night my Mother-in-law,
 Spent hours talking about her toe nails,
And then about how her husband fails…"
I shift in my seat, too much information,
Then I heard something about castration.
My ears pricked up,
Thank God, she was talking about her pup!
I suddenly notice something interesting,
'Mr Onion' has just been joined by that brunette,
who always smells of cigarettes.
I'd say, more than friends, but how can you tell?
Though she obviously doesn't have a sense of smell.
My mind continues to wander,
Off into the wild blue yonder….
"I've been deaf since having my face lift…"
That conversation sounds a gift,
But I have to get off the bus, before I'm stranded,
I've reached the end of my journey, I've landed.

Lis McDermott

UNSPOKEN THOUGHTS

The story you live in, is the story you live out.
Don't waste another second living in the past;
Live for now, don't run or hide away.

Don't be afraid, or allow fear to take control.
Only a small percent of fear will ever happen,
All there is to fear, is fear itself.

Be generous and kind;
Forgive quickly, don't allow unforgiveness
to spoil your day, or peace of mind.
Love doesn't remember past hurts, it turns
over a new page, destroying the old.

Carolyne Crawford

The Moment before the Moment

A SINGLE TEARDROP

Silence, except for Dad, rehearsing his speech.
Tension, emotions constrained on her special day.
The mirror reflects a perfectly made-up, anxious, pale face.

She lingers, gazing at the vision returning her stare;
False laughter, smiles no longer there.
Earlier Champagne failing to impart the desired effect.
Whatever happened to her dreams?

Was it his hurtful comments, or fierce bursts of temper, when they didn't agree?
Fear takes hold, gripping tight;
Too late for doubts, must proceed, do what is right.
A sleek, black, shiny limousine awaits.

Exquisite, goddess like, in the bright summer sun;
White gossamer veil glistening, floating in light, cooling breeze.
Into the car she's lovingly led;
Dad whispers, "darling, tell me, are you sure you want to go ahead."

A single teardrop falls down a flawless cheek;
The moment before the moment that will determine her destiny.
Dad declares, "Driver, don't stop, take a detour, drive a few
more times around the block".

                        Carolyne Crawford

THE MOMENT BEFORE THE MOMENT

In the rising heat of the early morning sun,
students and children, worked,
demolishing bombed buildings.
Fire and wood mix far too well,
Every building, home, school work place,
born of trees.
The spotters had already searched the skies,
The all clear given.

We children played in streets,
My mother kept me with her,
wherever she went, I was her shadow.
My brother was riding his bike,
His feet free of shoes.
My sister ran after a dragonfly fluttering on
the warm breeze…

Eight-fifteen all the clocks stopped dead,
Nobody had expected Enola Gay.

                    Lis McDermott

Writing about a Unique Talent
You may or may not Possess

MUSICAL DREAMING

Magical, musical dreaming delight;
Listening day or night,
Relaxing, preferably at home,
Playing music on DVD or radio.
Exhilarating, transporting, when alone.

Captivating melodies, sounds of Mozart,
Beethoven, Rachmaninov, Bach.
Senses drawn down mysterious paths;
Triggering powerful emotions, tears.
Reminders of places, people, loves of the past.

Dreams of fame, performing solo piano, violin.
Eyes closed, wishful dreaming can
take you almost anywhere;
allow you to do anything.
Remember to cherish the applause.

Carolyne Crawford

SEA WHISPERER

When tides are low, and ripples of sand are visible
I whisper to the sea shells, to the gentle ebb and flow,
Leaning down, my lips above the brine,
I whisper words of magic; of watery tales,
Sagas of star fish, turning luminescent,
Shedding light on the cerulean waters,
Illuminating the blues and greens for sea-horse knights,
as they glide and flow on their quest,
disappearing, elegantly into the depths.
In rockpools I duet with mermaids,
Crooning lilting lullabies for the young of the ocean deep,
calling them home to sleep -
before the incoming storm clouds gather,
and the raging waves crash and break
on the craggy rocks and pebbles of the beach.
I whisper my melodies on the gentle ebb and flow…and ebb and flow…

       Lis McDermott

Christmas and Festive

SANTA'S CHRISTMAS VISIT

'Twas the night before Christmas;
Four excited children frolic, around a sparkling, festive tree,
Chanting, "Ho, Ho, Ho, hurray! Tonight, Santa's coming, with presents for you, and me."

They intend to feign sleep, to greet him,
Welcome Santa with sherry, mince pies.
Maybe he'll get stuck down the chimney?
Using Santa magic, he'll fit, just fine.
Uncharacteristically easy, with angelic smiles, into bed they all climb.

Later, all awake with a start,
"Have we missed Santa?
In cold darkness, on tippy toe, they creep;
Aware of the stairs that creek.
Anxious to be first, they claw, push, shove;
Tangle together in a heap, of arms, legs, feet.

Small hands fumble, on pops the light;
Eyes widen, jaws drop, faces transfixed with surprise;
An Aladdin's cave of delight, comes into sight.
Scooters, dolls, books, teddies, games, toy trains.
Santa's been exceedingly busy tonight.

Stop! Footsteps sound on the stairs.
Door opens, all turn around;
"Happy Christmas monkeys," Daddy declares.
"You should be counting sheep."
Giggles, smiles, he looks really odd without his false teeth and half asleep.

Carolyne Crawford

CHRISTMAS DAY

Childish memories linger still
How the thought of gifts he will bring
Rolling in the white, wet snow
Icy flakes the wind doth blow
Santa in his sleigh we hope to see
The early nights too excited to sleep
Mom and Dad telling us to be quiet
At last Christmas Day it as aspired
Shall we be happy with all we get
Do we want more than just a pet
As the excitement fades away
You eagerly wait another Christmas Day

Ann Brady

HOLLY

Much favoured on festive shopping lists.
Prickly, glossy, oval, evergreen leaves;
Stunning, scarlet berries, complete the show.
Dressing the halls with garlands of holly, enhance,
brighten any home, usually paired off with Ivy.
Together, in folklore, used to ward off evil spirits;
Celebrate new growth.

Carolyne Crawford

Dear Santa,

For Christmas, please can I have:
My own unicorn, so I can jump over rainbows,
One of those glass bubbles - when shaken, it snows;
A new pair of bright red, sneakers, or pumps
they'll help me leap much higher when I jump.
A black cat that can talk to me, so I'm not alone
when Mum and Dad leave me behind at home.
New glasses for my best friend, Leigh
because at the moment, she just can't see;
Anything from Grandma that isn't pink,
I may be a girl, but that colour just stinks!
I know it's a tall order, but a new little brother or sister,
because since our Jenny went away, I really miss her.
I know sometimes I'm naughty, misunderstood,
But I promise, I'll do my best to be good.

                                      Lis McDermott

Falling from the Sky

THE SHEPHERDS STORY

In the velvet darkness of night,
Myriads of bright stars, sparkled,
lighting the sky.
The cold night, dispelled all clouds,
and one by one the stars fell from the sky,
showering the earth with luminous
brilliance, illuminating the souls of men;
Each heavenly body died as they touched the earth.
They prepared the way;
In the heavens above, a new celestial being emerged;
One, dazzling, intensely shining star,
appearing in the heavy blackness.
It's fierce glow, hovering over one spot on earth.
We, and many others were drawn to the place,
and there witnessed a king's birth.

                      Lis McDermott

TEARDROPS

Gentle as teardrops, slowly they fall
Hitting the ground and the wall
Disappearing as if they've never been here
Perhaps because they are too sheer

But as the temperature goes on down
They prance and dance like a clown
We run and laugh, holding our hands out wide
We try to catch them and are mystified

Where do they go, why don't they stay?
All we want to do, is to have some fun and play.
But still the snowdrop disappears
And we are left with just our tears

Ann Brady

STARS FALLING FROM THE SKY

The first moment man gazed up into the heavens,
He's been fascinated by the grandeur,
 splendour of countless, shimmering, sparkling, blinking stars.
Fairy lights, beautifully illuminated against velvet, ink black, night skies.

Often seeming like snowfall, glistening in outer space;
Magnificent displays of falling stars;
Tiny bits of dust, rock, known as meteors, rapidly moving, burning up, high in the sky.
Flashing, fiery streaks, silently falling down to Earth.

Reminiscent of Perry Como, in surreal moments, we're tempted to reach out;
'Catch a falling star, put it in our pocket, save it for a rainy day.'
Sometimes we are like stars;
We fall to make someone's wish, dream, come true.

      Carolyne Crawford

Words Inspired by a picture

HAPPY DAYS

I've been this way before;
In chilly spring, summer heat,
autumn mist, winter sleet.
Bad-tempered gulls, screeching overhead.
Days of joyous freedom,
Childish pent-up energy released.

Laughing, cheeks rosy, running wellie-clad,
along narrow, precarious, stony cliff paths;
Stopping at the headland, away from
the crumbling, chalky cliff edge.
Your warning, "don't go too far,"
lost on the chilly, breezy north wind.

Silver sea glistening in the distance;
We descend steep, slippery steps,
to dark, mysterious rock pools, exposed
at low tide, on the wet seashore.
Excitement, anticipation mounts;
What treasures await today?

You sit, sentinel like, on your favourite rock,
Thermos in hand, surveying my every move.
I glance, you smile, wave;
Reassured you're still there, I'm lost in my world
Of make-believe, of swashbuckling pirates,
pieces of eight.

I climb over slimy, smelly, seaweed covered rocks;
Seeking small crabs, star fish, cast-off shells.
Searching for shiny, coloured stones, sea glass;
Polished over time by angry, pounding seas.
Seemingly hours pass, I can hear your call,
"Home now, it's time for tea".

Years have flown, I walk this way alone.
Mum, in this place you are forever young;
I can hear our laughter, see your smile.
I'll always cherish memories of our happy
days, time spent playing amongst rocks,
beside the sparkling sea.

Carolyne Crawford

Inspiration: a holiday photo of the seaside.

There is something surreal about a woman
doing nothing, leisurely at ease.
I feel inclined to ask – sorry, Miss,
but are all the chores done?
I wasn't expecting this,
mostly because you *are* a woman.

Can you imagine – if she turned to say,
no, it is my time now to read,
to hang from the sofa should it please me.
Oh, the blasphemy.

I'd feel rather perplexed at how this could be,
and ask her once more, forcefully -
what are your intentions for the house and for the
meals that must be consumed by your husband
and your kids?
Don't you think it's a little out of hand
to ignore your responsibilities towards those that
continuously demand and take?

She might turn me away with a wave of her hand.
I'm on a break – she might say – and I intend to take
as long as I need to feel pleasure.

I wasn't built to serve. I was designed to create.
I was created to exist. And exist I shall, in leisure.

Greeshma Rajeev

Inspiration: David Hettinger's art series that explores the lives of women reading, and at leisure

She leans towards the fragrant
blossom, gently fondling its petals,
A bee settles close by, sucking nectar,
droplet by droplet,
in the heat of the summer sun;
She innocently inhales, and sighing
releases a whispered breath
that sets my heart racing;
I crave her scent, long to caress
the translucent, pure skin
of her virginal breasts;
Like a moth to a flame, I am drawn to her;
with no escape, I am lost

Lis McDermott

Inspiration: a photograph of a bride, with her back to the photographer, leaning in to smell blossom

New Year

THE NEW YEAR LOOKING FORWARD

Looking into the future
We think and plan our way
And yet we should not be surprised
When the opposite comes into play

It will not matter what you want
You'll only achieve your goals
If you set your heart and minds upon
the task at hand, forgetting all your woes

For life cannot be dictated to
You should always be aware
That what's around the corner
Is really meant to be there

So gird your loins as warriors do
And face this coming New Year
With strength and stamina and all you have
Without sustaining fear.

Ann Brady

Never in modern history has there been a greater catastrophe;
Every nation traumatised by a virus with high mortality,
Worldwide suffering, feelings of fear, depression, anxiety.
Yearlong endurance, lockdowns, loss of livelihood, personal fatality.
Eventually vaccines bring hope for future return to normality;
Although early days, vaccinations commence globally.
Ramifications, effects of the virus, will remain indefinitely.

                        Carolyne Crawford

NEW CALENDAR

Timeworn calendar of yesteryear
I gladly finally binned today.
Rid myself of all its dust, and
its stink of abysmal dismay.

> Crisp aroma of a brand-new book, or
> petrichor under cerulean yonder
> freshly unburdened of dark clouds,
> so smells the hope in my new calendar.

Between the leaves of upcoming months,
would be wrapped myriad stars.
Some would light our path ahead
and others, liberate us of old scars.

> And dirt? Oh! that won't settle around
> when we vroom through with a new pace.
> In almanac doodled with to-do lists,
> vigour will claim back its place.

Naman Kumar

Haiku about interesting words

SCRUMPTIOUS

The cat licks her lips;
Fishy was truly scrumptious,
His tank stands empty.

Blond hair and blue eyes;
A scrumptious combination.
Good enough to date.

Don't linger too long.
Dinner is scrumptious tonight;
Soon it'll be all gone.

Scrumptious birthday cake,
A decorated delight.
Hidden out of sight.

        Carolyne Crawford

PANDEMIC
I miss the world when
pandemics were endemic
in history texts, not news

BROUHAHA
Some people I meet
are gatherings in themselves –
one-man brouhaha

POST-COVID WEDDING
A masked afternoon
at the city hall, quiet
matrimonial.

HAIKU
Where syllables speak,
getting lost in a haiku
has its own magic.

MISSION
Before youth departs,
I hope my heart has found a
purpose, a mission.

        Greeshma Rajeev

COLLYWOBBLES
My poor stomach feels
Very upset, queasy, full
Of collywobbles

Collywobbles sounds
Like a great description for
Walking on cobbles!

CAPRICIOUS
Don't be capricious,
First you say it's delicious,
Then it's disgusting.

Your mood changes drive
Me insane with your sudden,
Wild capriciousness.

                    Lis McDermott

KEMEREBI
Struggles embellish.
Trees hinder sunlight, create
Fine Kemerebi.

               Naman Kumar

*Kemerebi – Japanese expression for the sunlight as it filters through the trees.

Slow Poison

On the Richter scale of relationships,
as innocuous as it may feel,
even the faintest of earthquakes
emanating from
doubt,
confusion,
frustration
and discord,
grows exponentially
and causes Tsunamis,
sweeping off the love that once was.

What then remain
are hollow but heavy moments
forcing us to gulp
bitter pills of truth,
day in day out,
venomous to head and heart,
robbing life of lives –
the sun sets in broad daylight,
the moon never rises,
and all that's left of
once soul-enriching nectar
is life-threatening slow poison.

    Naman Kumar

I know just when it started
That feeling of despair
When I found my breathing laboured
Each time I climbed the stairs

The stress it finally got me
My hair began to fall
As I sat and waited eagerly
For the moment he would call

I questioned all my senses
The room was odourless
I dare not move too far from home
The world appeared so colourless

I thought that he did love me
He seemed so quite sincere
And yet all he ever wanted
Was revenge for all these years

And so, it has finally hit me
My head begins to hum
The painful feelings overtaking me
Have been caused by the poison, Thallium

                        Ann Brady

Darkly sinister, stealthy silent;
Rampant worldwide injustice, racism,
corruption, crimes of hate combine to
wreak havoc, wreck innocent lives.
Incited by social media, slowly poison
an unmindful world today.
Time to take account, halt complacency.
Matters most urgent, will not go away.
Sadly, the transition from chaos to utopia,
is unlikely to happen overnight.

                        Carolyne Crawford

Sadly, fascism is gaining a hold on the political stage
Disquietly seeping into the world like a slow poison,
Their right-wing beliefs growing like any other plague,
Sadly, fascism is gaining a hold on the political stage.
Conflict in populations, hampers opportunities to politely engage,
Is this the road to democracy's erosion?
Sadly, fascism is gaining a hold on the political stage,
Disquietly seeping into the world like a slow poison

                          Lis McDermott

My Love is Like….

A PERFECT LOVE

My love is your love, your love is my love.
Quick as a flash, 50 years have passed.
For better or worse, through good times and bad,
Like the sun, my love continues to shines on you.
Over time, first passionate love, has matured like
fine wine, into a sweet, fragrant, steady kind.
My love adores every wrinkle, line on your age worn
face;
Your brown, curly hair, peppered with grey.
Your lovely smile, that lights up the room,
I love watching you nap away the afternoon.
I even love your silly jokes, they brighten up a dreary
day.
With age comes wisdom;
Though my love isn't perfect, it's as strong as the
wind.
It never fails, gives up, walks away.

                              Carolyne Crawford

My love is….

A cup of tea to quench my thirst
Opening the door to let me go first
A gentle grip upon my hand
Upon my finger a wedding band

My love is this
But much more than that.
I love him because, he lets me wear
His fedora hat!

                Ann Brady

My love is like… a good fitting glove.

Opening the mail after the postman has called
Wondering how much he has left in the hall.
Where do the letters or postcards come from?
Is it America, Australia, maybe Sierra Leone

It doesn't really matter who has written to me
Because all I ever want is some writing to see.
Those words that are written on the paper so neat
Are ecstatic to me, such a powerful treat.

The words enter my mind, being almost biblical
As I devour and absorb each letter and syllable.
Where did we learn this craft so delightful
Of placing down squiggles that charm, or are spiteful?

We write with gay abandon, a mind-set full of determination,
Never worrying or caring for correct punctuation.
And then we are done, our words are concluded
Finished at last, as we no longer feel secluded.

Into an envelope we entrust our thoughts and dreams.
It's all meant to be part of that ever-larger scheme,
Of sharing our views, our fears, and our love,
For writing for me, is like wearing a good fitting glove.

                         Ann Brady

My love is like….

Waiting for the sun to rise in the sky,
Catching my breath with its beauty.
My love is like
Rippling waves of the sea,
Continually dancing over shingle.
My love is like
Warmth, cocooned within an everlasting embrace,
Dewdrops of rain, falling gently on my face.
My love is like
A trapeze act, flying through the air,
Knowing the other will always be there.
My love is like inhaling oxygen each day,
Completely accepting me, my heart, my way.

Lis McDermott

Beauty is Everywhere

OPEN YOUR EYES

Open your eyes, tell me what you see?
Is it a rich blue sky or a buzzing bee?
Maybe a tree from which wild flowers hang
Swaying in the wind, imagine if they sang?
Look at the fish swimming by in the lake so green.
Or at the birds who sit and slowly preen.
What about the frog who croaks and calls to you?
Look up at the eagle who has a lofty view.
Feel the raindrops falling one by one.
Hear them tip, tap, gently on the pond.
The sound of the gravel as you're walking along,
Scuffing your shoes as if singing a song.
Remember there is beauty, all around, everywhere.
All you have to do, is to stop, listen and stare.

                                        Ann Brady

LONDON

Taking an evening walk by the river,
The shadows cast by the moon
create a hinterland of silhouettes,
Standing guard, linked by their uniformity,
streetlights, twinkling-reflections in the Thames;
Millennium Bridge, leads to the dome of St Paul's
paying homage in its shapely structure,
paving the way for the majestic, ancient architecture,
The power-station-tower of Tate Modern,
looms, silent and watchful in the surrounding
blackness.
Tower blocks, like glittering light installations
blaze in the sky, adding an artificial
glow to the darkness of night;
The Thames, meanders, the waters washing
over its bank, causing boats to rock, creak,
bump against the quay,
Creating a rhythmic accompaniment
to the distant, muffled sounds of traffic,
As people disappear homeward bound.
Breathing deeply inwards, I inhale the beauty
of this living city.

                              Lis McDermott

BEAUTY IS EVERYWHERE

Wonder of wonders,
There is beauty everywhere.
Everything has beauty,
Not everyone sees it.
Search near, far, find it in your
dreams, in laughter, smiles,
Hidden in dark corners of your mind.
Beauty in the eyes of the beholder
Is everywhere.
Find it in love, use it for ultimate good.
See beauty in dramatic, orange, red sunsets,
transforming into romantic, silvery, moonlit nights.
In spectacular gardens, overflowing with fragrant,
exotic blooms, in multi-coloured hues.
Chattering, noisy birdsong, rudely awakening the
day.
Soothing, captivating music, caressing stress away.
In panoramic, black velvet, twinkling, starry night
skies.
Carpets of delicate snowdrops, gracefully bowing
their white-capped heads, in virgin snow.
Writing inspiring poetry, stories, enriching thoughts.
In beautiful people with beautiful minds;
Beauty shining from without and within.

Close your eyes, celebrate treasured,
beautiful memories coming alive.
Reflect on the beauty of freedom,
Rediscover beauty in peace, love.

                    Carolyne Crawford

Mother

I WANT TO GO HOME

'Twas the night before Xmas, I'm thinking of home
As I lay in the darkness, I feel all alone.
I think of my Mother, sitting still in the chair
Her face will look sad, because I'm not there.

I want to go home, but I'm far, far away
As under this palm tree, I silently lay.
The night it is cold, the desert is black
The silence shouts out at me, but I mustn't shout back.

I think of the Xmas tree, Mother up in the loft has sought
How gaily it will shine, with the baubles she's bought.
The presents she'll wrap, in paper so gay
And put under the tree, like fallen leaves they will lay.

The guns they start firing, I'm frozen with fear
So I think of that Xmas tree and my Mother so dear.
I reach out my hand, but she is not there
I don't understand why the place seems so bare.

The silence surrounds me,
I let out a groan
My time it is ended,
So now I'll go home.

        Ann Brady

AN INEVITABLE METAMORPHOSIS

I am slowly transforming into my mother.
The soft, fleshy upper arms she used to hate,
and I used to poke when I needed something,
they are growing on me of late.

There are deepening, darkening bulbs
right underneath my sleepy eyes.
There are times when I'm brushing my teeth
and the mirror takes me by surprise.

I start my day, like she did, with yoga and meditation,
a plethora of exercises designed to calm me.
I never thought I would believe in prayer
but there are too many things now that alarm me.

In equal parts, I find vigor and joy and warmth,
and the wish to do something more with her life.
It feels like I've stumbled into a stranger's garden
where she made sure to plant little flowers of bright

amongst the weeds of the unavoidable mundane,
a sort of ray of sunshine in the depths of the night.
In me too, I find, a yearning, a romance,
tiny pulses of peonies in the midst of all the strife.

Every time I get angry at something she would,
I want to turn back the clock and ask for forgiveness.
I am finally beginning to understand a version of my mother,
thanks to this inevitable metamorphosis.

                                              Greeshma Rajeev

MOTHER

Mother, do you know how your love
Bolstered me, when growing up?
Knowing I was loved unconditionally,
Feeling safe and secure each day,
Supported in a happy home?

Even when I left home for college,
You still held me in your influence
As though I lived in your shadow,
Scared of making serious mistakes,
In the chance I might upset you,

Vicariously, you lived out your dreams
Through my career path,
Yet, still your dominance managed to
Overshadow me from maturing;
Too long, I was held in your sway,

Unable to break the umbilical cord,
Even having moved away,
Until I met the love of my life,
Displeased you for my choices,
Spread my wings and flew.

Even in your later years,
When, I had a career of my own building,
You reminded me regularly
How it was your work that paved the way,
But for you, I wouldn't be who I am.

Mother, I love you still,
Yet, I have flourished in my life,
Yes, with seeds sown by you,
But watered and fed by my own
Creativity and ability.

I hope you see I have become
The woman I am, both,
because of you and despite you.
I love you, and always will,
but glad to be set free, to be me

      Lis McDermott

MY MOTHER

Mother, what a dear, sweet name;
I can picture you now in my mind;
Your adorable laugh, sparkling, sunny smile,
The best mother anyone could hope to find.
Only a generous heart of gold like yours,
Would lay down her life for me.
Tirelessly working day and night;
Nurturing, teaching, cooking, cleaning,
Making my life happy, carefree, bright.
How could I ever thank you enough for
Showering me with your perfect love.
I miss your gentle kiss goodnight,
Your loving touch when we cuddled,
Snuggled tight.
Endlessly encouraging, you kept faith,
When I floundered, lost my way.
Like a sculptor you crafted me into the
Confident person, I am today.
Richly blessed is how I feel, to have known,
Loved, an amazing mother like you.

                        Carolyne Crawford

My Eden

The time will come when I'll walk alone
With no-one by my side
But I will not be hurried
Nor allow myself to be worried

And though my years are numbered
And my life is slowing down
As I walk I'll swing and sway
As I go along my lonely pathway

For life is what you make of it
Whether it be good or bad
You choose to walk, to run or fly
And whether to laugh or cry

And when I lay my head upon
The softness of my pillow
I know at last to my Eden I've been led
It's the warmth and comfort of my bed.

                Ann Brady

Watching the reflection
Of a seascape in your eyes,
Whish and hush,
Whish and hush;
Walking beside the
Rippling ebb and flow,
Trickling gently over the sand,
Whish and hush,
Whish and hush;
Tasting your salty lips
As we kiss,
The breeze blowing our hair,
Whish and hush,
Whish and hush;
Every breath I inhale
Brings peace
Whish.......

        Lis McDermott

MY EDEN

Sometimes I visit an imaginary place,
Within the confines of my mind.
Where the golden sun forever shines,
The cloudless sky is luminous blue,
And the tranquil, sapphire sea sparkles,
Like polished glass in the sun.
I walk tirelessly for miles along a
Sun drenched, white sandy beach,
Lined with elegant, tall coconut palms;
Their swaying, rustling fronds softly
Whisper to me, as I pass by.
I love the feeling of the cool, refreshing,
Foaming surf, splashing over my feet.
The sound of waves, gently lapping the
Sea shore, soothes my troubles away.
A glorious feeling of freedom descends;
I'm blissfully happy, as free as a bird,
In my idyllic, enchanting paradise.

                              Carolyne Crawford

Self-Portrait

I stare into the mirror
And am shocked at what I see
Is that my hair upon my head?
Or maybe a bushy tree?
The hair is down below my collar.
I need to get it cut.
My sideburns they are now so long,
Ribbons in them I can put.
As I look at my hair
My mind it wanders far.
As I suddenly burst into song,
I'm singing like a country star!
Is it Shania, or Loretta Lyn,
Dolly, Tammy or perhaps Patsy Cline?
Whoever it is, who's vocalising,
She's certainly singing out in rhyme.
My eyes they clear, I focus in
At the bluish bush upon my nut.
I shake my head and tell myself
Girl, you really do need to get your hair cut!

Ann Brady

THAT'S ME

I'm the lynchpin of my family;
A quintessential busy bee.
Flitting here, there, everywhere,
Finding no time to sit or stare.
Working hard all the day,
In a purposeful, pleasant way.
Where would our world be today,
Without the cute, buzzing bee,
And me?

Carolyne Crawford

MY INNER CAT

Taking an afternoon nap, stretched out on my bed,
nuzzling into the pillows,
satisfies my inner cat.
To the one's I love, I promise loyalty and friendship
unadulterated.
Show me affection and I will follow you,
to the ends of the earth,
as long as you feed me fish,
particularly salmon!
If you cross me, my claws will emerge,
sharp and viciously prepared for action,
Though this is rare, more likely, often than not,
if you offend my mate.
My hair, as silky and soft as that of a British Blue,
chokes when wisps find their way into your mouth;
With age, I have become more aloof;
rather than argue, I'll lick my paws,
turn and walk away.
When I don't want to engage,
I'll curl up and read a good book,
When happy, I loudly purr,
humming with contentment.

                            Lis McDermott

Haiku

Entitled:
Bird Song
My Heart Feels
Looking out of the Window
A quiet Moment
Morning Walk

BIRD SONG
Songstress of the night,
Sing to me, I know you're there,
My sweet nightingale.

MY HEART FEELS
My heart sings, it beats,
It aches, breaks, it soars, it longs
For you, only you.

LOOKING OUT THE WINDOW
Thunder, rain clearing,
Sun peeking through stormy clouds.
Happiness, delight.

A QUIET MOMENT
Take a well-earned break,
Enjoy coffee, squishy cake.
Relax, take a nap.

MORNING WALK
Blue skies, birds chorus,
Fragrant blossom in the air.
Elated I stride.

     Carolyne Crawford

Chirping, cheerful sounds
Wake me; music to my ears
Beautiful birdsong

My heart feels complete
Elation when I hear my
Name falls from your lips.

Through the window
The woodpigeons coo and call
Perched in their oak tree.

A quiet moment
When my breath becomes your breath,
Our hearts beat as one.

Early morn walks, the
Light glimmers through the trees in
A misty sunrise

       Lis McDermott

A QUIET MOMENT - ON MEDITATION
Reach for the spaces
between breathing in and out;
slow down the traffic.

THROUGH THE WINDOW AT NIGHTTIME
Little yellow squares
small muted people, cooking,
cleaning, and living.

BIRD SONG
Say, how come you have
so much to say at sunrise,
yet I am silent?

I like to listen,
it comforts me – life goes on
even when I can't.

MY HEART FEELS - ON ALLOWING CHANGE

It is foolishness
that claims loss can make or break.
We are much bigger.

MORNING WALK – OPTIMISM

Isn't it silly,
the Sun's dramatic entry?
He knows night will come.

                Greeshma Rajeev

THROUGH MY WINDOW
As through my window I look
The world is in torment
Will I still exist
Tomorrow Morn'
Can I see
No, I'm
Gone.

MY HEART FEELS
As you take my hand in yours
I feel your warmth touch me
Surround me with your
Gentle breathing
Touch my cheek
My heart
Feels.

A QUIET MOMENT
Is this a Quiet Moment?
A sound of nothingness
Meant to sooth me mind
Shall I cry out
to disturb
this peace
No

BIRD SONG
Listening to the Bird's Song
Brings joy unto your ears
Warmth surrounds your soul
Smiles cross your face
Close your eyes
Sing and
Fly.

Morning Walk
It's an early morning walk
By the river you tread
Fish swim in water
Waves call to you
One step near
You drop
Within.
              Ann Brady

Not Haiku, but Ann's own creation.

Fool

FOOL

A bait to a fish
is what your smile is
to me.
I strive to spot
the hook,
but it's all blurred,
indiscernible
behind your crook.
One glance of yours
washes my wisdom away,
I get back to square one
where you never stay.

I fear not falling
for you, over 'n' over,
but only
being fooled again.

                      Naman Kumar

HOW TRUE

A fool and his money are easily parted;
I'm mortified, aghast at my stupidity,
Desperately trying hard to keep my cool.
Why on earth did I answer the phone?
I wish I'd gone out, not stayed home.
Sadly, I was convinced by his genuine,
Authoritative tone.
I should have stopped, used my head,
Listened with care to all he said.
Now he's stolen all my money,
I'm humiliated, too embarrassed to tell.
Wholeheartedly, I curse and damn the
Abominable, scammer to hell.

                        Carolyne Crawford

A FOOLS SONG

Am I the fool as I stand and watch you walk away
Sighing deeply, sadness encompassing me?
Will you no longer be by my side?
Is this the way my life is now to be?

I cannot find the words to say,
What will express my deepest gloom,
For as I turned you closed the door,
Leaving me in this cold dark room.

I should have told you long ago
How I knew you had done me wrong,
But my lips remained tightly closed,
A misbegotten fool singing to the wrong song.

                              Ann Brady

The clown of the classroom is often misunderstood,
Wanting to play it cool, but in fact, acting the fool
Covering hidden, hurtful damage with a grin,
Many clowns laugh on the outside, but cry within.

Comedians are often serious people offstage,
The sad clown paradox, being allowed out of the box
Many, suffering from hideous depression
Yet seek validation in this mad profession

Most of us are caught out, fools at some time in our lives
Becoming naïve, only too ready to believe
in someone or something, or misguided notions
Seriously messing with our heart's emotions.

       Lis McDermott

Reflections

REFLECTIONS OF YOU

Reflections of you and me;
The way life used to be, two hearts
Beating as one, in perfect harmony.
Of carefree, blissful, star filled nights,
Strolling hand in hand along the shore.
Silvery moonbeams casting shadows,
Illuminating your handsome face.
Romantic, intimate dinners for two,
At our favourite eating place.
Living the ultimate dream, both riding
High on a breath-taking wave of love.

Our relationship wasn't destined to be;
My heart broke into a million pieces
When you chose her, not me
I miss our life and how you made me
Feel more alive each day,
We laughed, loved the hours away.
I thought you were my 'one true love'.
We'd be together forever, living a
'Happily-ever-after' fairy tale life.
I would walk to the ends of the
Earth to be back in your arms.

Alas, I'm alone, stuck in limbo in a
Dark, desolate place, with only
Memories to ease my pain.
Friends tell me I should move on;
I've been hiding away for too long,
I must start afresh, have some fun!
Stop reflecting on the why, where, how?
Given time my feelings of loss will fade;
It's not a sign of weakness,
It's a passage, not a place to stay,
It is the price of love, I have to pay.

      Carolyne Crawford

REFLECTIONS

The call of the sea is beckoning me as I tenderly make my way,
My toes sink into soft sand as memories rise from long ago.
Here am I venturing, onwards through the rocky cliff sides,
Wondering where it would lead me? Maybe to a time of my youth.
'Ouch, ouch, ouch,' I say out loud as my feet tread the rocky outcrop.
Suddenly I can see my goal with the sun shining bright and bold.
Tenderly I pick my way over the sharpened shards of rock
And there stretched out before me was the feeling I thought I'd lost.
When only a child I remembered the days spent out in the sun,
Of sand castles, swimming and laughter until the day was done,
And here I am once again remembering all I'd lost.
So, I soaked myself in the moment, recalling happy childhood years.

Ann Brady

Reflections are what we see in the world,
Each day, wanting to see contentment not
Fear, yet we all seem to be scared of our
Lives becoming dominated by government rules.
Escape into the freedom of your own mind and
reflect,
Concentrate on communicating with other humans,
Together in kindness, we can move forward,
Inhabit this world with fresh eyes,
Optimistically, build a new caring world,
Not one of selfish abandon, but in commune by
Smiling into the hearts of those we meet.

                Lis McDermott

OLD FRIENDS ARE MADE AT A YOUNG AGE

We spend so long looking for romance
because we think we're supposed to,
because we think everyone else is.
We find ourselves caught in this deep desire
to love and be loved,
yet somehow, we all end up alone.
Ants in a formation that just doesn't lead home.

We've made the wrong things important –
the job, the house, the need to appear put together,
the waistline and the race to the finish line -
and we've forgotten what it used to be like
when we lay with the wind rubbing against our bare calves,
on patches of green, a summer reprieve
with friends we were certain were our other halves.
When the conversation ran out,
we basked in the silence,
the Sun heavy on our eyelids,
talking us into an afternoon slumber.

Remember how we complained then
about how alone we were?

Greeshma Rajeev

Poems using the Pleiades Form

SUMMER

Sunshine like powdered gold,
Sparkling on swaying corn.
Sweet scented roses bloom,
Senses swoon in delight.
Soft, warm, summer breezes,
Sunsets smeared in deep red,
Stifling hot, humid nights.

                    Carolyne Crawford

WINTER

Welcome, warmy zephyr!
With you nowhere in sight,
winter took its chances,
withering me again,
waned all my hopes for light.
We hold on and win, or
wear just a wistful grin.

                    Naman Kumar

FAITH

Finders, keepers, healers
Fascinating teacher
Fearless with lots of hope
Functional to some souls
Fashionable to more
Fanatics, look within
Forgive sinners who sin

                      Greeshma Rajeev

FEATHERS

Floating down from the trees,
Fluffy, soft, adding warmth,
Fragile in their beauty,
Fancy colour-displays
Fabulous peacock blues
Frayed and tattered, midst flight
Found, removed, suggesting
Fallen angels are near.

                      Lis McDermott

**I Bloomed in your embrace
like Daffodils in Spring.**

Throughout the cold, frosty nights of winter
we were parted, shivered alone with our sorrows,
seemingly abandoned by the warmth of our love.
With the change of seasons, encouraged
by the chance of meeting, when we spoke,
my heart thrived at the sound of your voice,
The encouraging tone of your words,
When we met, I felt as though your light
had shone on me, energising my whole being,
Allowing my fragile soul to once again flourish,
I bloomed in your embrace like daffodils in spring.

                                        Lis McDermott

YOU'RE MINE

For me there is no other,
In your arms I wish to stay.
Your smile brings me joy and
Your laughter lights my way.
You are the cure for my darkness,
You are the air I breathe,
The bright star I gaze.
I bloomed in your embrace
Like a daffodil in spring.
You are everything to me.

     Carolyne Crawford

ACHE OF SAUDADE

From a still to a throbbing heart
only you could ever bring,
I bloomed in your embrace
like daffodils in spring.

As the luminance of the Summer,
Or the vibrance of the Fall,
Even the best lacks your essence
that gets me enthralled.

Enduring the ache of saudade -
bone-breaking and nerve-racking,
Hanging fire for your one more touch
not dreading my end of being.

As a seed, dead-wrapped with soil,
I'll be lying somewhere around,
muted, yearning for your return,
to grow again in the ground.

                      Naman Kumar

Saudade is a Portuguese word that means, a feeling of longing, melancholy or nostalgia.

Harmony

HARMONY

Flocks of starlings
flying in waves of
whirling yet synced shapes,
many-hued dusk
turning the turquoise sea
kaleidoscopic,
the breeze on the beach
besotted by my beloved
caressing us to comfort
in a summer twilight,
her hands in mine,
I look into her eyes, and
in that very moment,
my otherwise dissonant life
and everything it comprises
play together
in a tuneful harmony.

     Naman Kumar

Happiness transpires when we unify to give
peace a chance,
Acting quickly to resolve conflicts fairly, and
positively.
Relationships blossom when people unite in
forgiveness, and love,
Maintain a healthy, optimistic outlook on life.
Out of bitterness and resentment, friendships
are promptly restored.
Nice people radiate 'good vibes', creating positive
emotions, righteous thoughts.
You, and I can transform the world, by consciously
acting in truth and love.

                                          Carolyne Crawford

HARMONY

An eternity ago, we used to meet
in living rooms and patios,
in dedicated centres,
where our voices would chant together
ebbing and flowing to the breath of our neighbour.

It's just me now,
sitting cross-legged, my laptop on the ground,
young, old, tanned faces squashed into square spaces,
strong in our unity, yet somehow all alone,
our mouths moving to the rhythm of
Nam Myoho Renge Kyo.

Out of sync is normal,
for internet connections waver
and some like to speed up
while others want to go slower.
Every few minutes, for a single moment,
these words, our breath, the pace –
it all comes together like it was meant to be.
The pandemic did its best and yet, here we are,
relentlessly grasping at harmony.

                              Greeshma Rajeev

HARMONY

Birds singing in the morning sun,
Although individual calls, their songs
join together, creating beautiful antiphony,
setting calmness for the whole day long.

Children's laughter is a wonderful sound,
High pitched, giggling like ringing bells
Making your heart rush with feelings of joy,
Rejuvenating your mind, casting youthful spells.

An array of colours to catch your eye, decorating
a wall as you walk by, captivated by its hues.
Artwork displayed for all to see and enjoy,
Greens, pinks, purples and glorious blues.

To meet that someone with whom you fit,
You share ideas, thoughts and dreams,
Are able to be completely yourself -
You have found your soulmate if seems.

Your personality tones are blended,
Together you are stronger than alone; a force
to be reckoned with, secure in your union,
For each other you are a happiness source.

Lis McDermott

Question and Answer…

TELL ME THE TRUTH ABOUT LOVE?

Poets and song writers famously declare,
'love is a many splendored thing.'
Always preferable to a 'one night' fling.
Human nature ordains, all people should seek the perfect mate,
Believe me, it's easier to leave the choice to fate.
In a heartbeat, love will strike like lightening out of the blue;
There is nothing to compare with the fluttery, butterfly, heart racing symptoms of falling head over heels in love, with someone new.
Feelings of 'happy anxiety' when you can't get a person out of your head,
Uneasy thoughts, loss of appetite, shyness, words left unsaid.
Love acts like a drug coursing through veins, causing euphoria, and passionate refrains.
Lovesick, desolate feelings, after lovers' part.
Love is caring, gentle, forgiving when conveying emotions, straight from the heart.
It is a priceless gift, to have and to hold;
Love is a treasure trove, worth more than gold.

The power of love chases away all doom and gloom,
from every house, in every room.
It is the essence of life, love is what makes our crazy
world go round,
its heavenly unity knows no bounds.

                        Carolyne Crawford

I WONDER

What will remain of me?
After these limbs
are laid to rest
to get one with the soil, and
the soul evaporates to ride
the canopy of clouds
beyond all the turmoil:

I know what will not stay -
certainly not what they see today,
nor what I want them to,
imploring them to see what's true.

May be as chlorophyll
flowing from the underground,
I'll be in the greens around,
or I'll rain down
to quench the thirst of the world
suffusing it with fragrant life-emeralds.

                Naman Kumar

HOW CAN WARS BE FOUGHT IN THE NAME OF RELIGION?

Varied beliefs; Muslim, Jew, Christian, Hindu, Sikh, Buddhist,
To different beings and gods in homage, so many pray,
Yet for some unearthly reason, unable to exist
in harmony, peacefully, side by side, living each day.
The faithful, hold fast to their tenets, their teachings and laws,
Truly believing their faith follows the only true God,
Preaching love and compassion, drawing others to their cause,
with an all-forgiving heart at the core. Is it not odd,
despite this religious devotion, establishments fight?
Casting doubt, spreading ill-will about the other doctrines,
Even dividing country bound'ries like the Golan Heights,
or make perceptions about the colour of converts skins.

How on earth can wars be fought in the name of religion?
In reality it's man who kills, creates division.

       Lis McDermott

Taking Inspiration from another poem…

RAGE AGAINST THE DYING LIGHT

As the first beam of dawn
sets the clock ticking
of a new day,
set forth and chase
your dream, as a leopard
does its prey.
Rage and race against
the dying light,
don't go gentle into
that good night.

For if you slow down,
let go of your grip, and
take a wrong turn at the fork,
from your sight it slips.
Lest you get trapped into
the restful twilight,
rage and race against
the dying light,
do not go gentle into
that good night.

Naman Kumar

Taking inspiration from the poem "Do not go gentle into that good night" by Dylan Thomas.

TRUE POEM

A true poem is birthed at its centre.
Like an afterthought, an exaltation,
the beginning and the end follow
once the middle achieves its gestation.

The middle is the crux, the clarity,
the reason why these words existed in us.
The true poem is the angry, scorching Sun,
and we, the poets, are all Icarus.

Rarely do we get to touch the realness,
the rawness of the metaphors we scribble down,
that is why of gut-wrenching, soul-crushing poetry,
there isn't enough to go around.

Yet, it is only in the trying and getting burnt
does mastery reside. We attempt to fly and realise
that Icarus was not failing as he fell,
he was discovering a new life in the skies.

Greeshma Rajeev

In response to Jack Gilbert's poem, "Failing and Flying"

THE DIARY OF A HOUSE CAT

Here amongst the dirty washing, cast-off
muddy trainers, boots and shoes,
Next door to the downstairs loo,
I take a well-earned boiler nap, in the
company of my washing, spinning,
drying friend.
Sometimes he does annoy, his swirling,
swishing, sloshing never seems to end.
To be fair, I'm a well-fed, pampered cat,
lovingly treated with care.
Although, my food I will not share.
I often jump up on Mum's lap and purr,
She loves to tickle, stroke my silky fur.
I journey far and wide to roam,
In a large area around my home.
Through gardens, meadows, fields of corn,
Sometime my antics cause neighbour's scorn.
With cunning stealth, I hunt, fixated on a
game of cat and mouse.
Afterwards, I carefully carry 'gifts' home,
for the people in our house.
I love to hear Mum's joyful scream,
Hunting is fun, it's all I know, and dream.

The audacity of next door's scrawny cat,
he infuriates me to the core,
> Flaunting, taunting, day and night,
> through our patio door.

No, it can't be, the most dreaded day
for every pet,
Our annual appointment with the vet.
I hiss, screech out loud, run like a cat out
of hell, immediately Mum gives chase,
Sadly, I never get to win the race.
"Come on," she yells, "it's not that far,"
With a vengeance I hate the vet, and
travelling in a cage, in the monster car.
It's been another full, exhausting day,
Time for a catnap, perchance to dream
of new adventures, not too far away.

    Carolyne Crawford

Loosely inspired by 'The Diary of a Church Mouse' by Sir John Betjeman.

Growing up, my aspirations were not mine,
They were the elusive hopes that you chased,
And fell short of in destination,
Yet still, unable to release your desires,
They were forced onto me, your child.
A generous parent would build bridges,
Forge mountains and remove all obstacles
For their offspring to blossom and grow;
Our relationship split into two,
And you talk on tiptoe, unable to be honest.
Only now, as I have met my matching soul,
Do I understand true altruistic love?
Though having hidden behind secret hopes
For these many years, I had to beseech him,
'Tread softly, because you tread on my dreams'
Needing to be sure, he fully understood
My life schemes.

                        Lis McDermott

Including words: "Tread softly, because you tread on my dreams" – W B Yeats and "And you talk on tiptoe" – Roger McGough

Midnight Lace

BLIND FEELINGS

Three times a day or more,
I tug at the creaky chain by my bed -
a village woman lifting up a pail of water -
bringing down the blinds,
often followed by a hurried changing
of pants and clasping of bras;
the squeak announcing when I leave the house,
return, shower, sleep,
shielding my swollen hips, coarse skin,
speckled breasts
from plain sight.

I wonder of the houses I peep into on my walks,
the ones with lavish curtains.
I imagine ballerinas floating up to the poles,
untying the perfectly framed cloth
with their perfectly lithe arms;
their mouths the colour of honeysuckle,
their skin the texture of silk,
their act of closing the curtains, foreplay.

I harbour their beauty in my eyes
each night, as I slowly lower my blinds

                    Greeshma Rajeev

MIDNIGHT LACE

Marshmallow clouds, float across the moon
like midnight lace,
Pulled gently across your beautiful face,
Shooting stars sprinkle glitter-dust in your
hair,
As I say an ever-thankful prayer
To the moon-goddess of night,
For gifting you to me from her glorious light.

                              Lis McDermott

THE DANCER

I saw her dancing there beneath the glowing,
mystical, full moon;
On a bright, starry summer's night,
I was captivated at first sight.
Her figure silhouetted by sparkling moonbeams,
filled with golden light.
An ethereal goddess, adorned in white.
In a trance-like state, she performed a celestial
repertoire of dance, pirouettes,
spinning, twirling, round and round.
Her beauty and grace held no bounds.
In the moonlight, intricate patterns of midnight lace,
delicately shone upon her radiant face.
I woke with a start, at the first hazy blush of dawn,
The dancer had vanished, without a trace.
I wonder was my phantom dancer real?
Or a vision of loveliness, transported from another
time, or place.

                          Carolyne Crawford

Word Flow

A Poetic form

BENEATH AND BEYOND

You, my rose, your petals I peel,
peeling away just the guard ones.
Beneath bruised husks, all it reveals,
revealing layers with blemishes none.

Battered by guests of tormenting moments,
momentarily they may feel incessant.
Your sturdy sanctum is a story of ascent,
ascending beyond their bounded laments.

Out in his orchard, you were born to bloom,
blooming as a flawless floret from within.
Oh, my love! Come along and discover,
discovering together your grace evergreen.

                          Naman Kumar

DAYLIGHT REVEALS REALITY TO ME

Lying in my bed, longing for sleep,
Sleeping alludes me, forever out of sight,
Awakes the horrors of darkness to seep,
Seeping from the fabric of night.

Visions of emptiness cause me to grieve,
Grieving for loved ones I pray not depart,
My life, desolate should they leave,
Leaving me solitary, breaking my heart.

My mind harried by these dreadful dreams,
Dreaming of futures, I'd rather not see,
In this half-light are secret lies it seems,
Seemingly, daylight will reveal reality to me.

                              Lis McDermott

All Shades of me

ALL SHADES OF ME

My favourite colour is everything in any shade of blue,
Some of you already know, the sea is my favourite view,
My language can sometimes be quite a colourful hue.
Twice in my life I've said those magical words, "I Do"
though the second time to my true love, through and through.
I have a great band of friends, the best ever crew.
Had my share of lovers, though never asked for a review.
I think my secrets would shock you - if only you knew.
I'm mostly, pretty level headed, don't think I'm a shrew…
People would probably say, I was a lot shyer, before I grew
into the woman you see now, old-age confidence anew.
There have been losses in my life, more than one or two,
family and friends who from this mortal coil and life flew.

I don't believe in fairies or ghosts – finding them a
                               bit too 'woo-woo',
Patience is within me for people, but gadgets get me
                               into a stew!
At times I'm sure people think I'm a little whacky
                               and cuckoo,
    To slow down, rest in peace, I'm certainly not
                               rushing to jump that queue.

                               Lis McDermott

It is truly a blessing to be a twin.
Surprisingly, her relocation gave me the opportunity to
discover the real me.
Above all things, my Christian faith is my world.
I'm a wife of many years, mother of two girls, doting grandmother
to six boys, all keep me on my toes, amused, happy and fit.
We're a close-knit family, who love to party,
enjoying life as it comes.
At heart I'm a proud Yorkshire lass, though Wiltshire is the place
I call home.
Long ago, I gave up being a perfectionist, experience has taught
me, life is too short.
I'm a lover of nature, the countryside, my lovely garden, animals,
birds and bees.
Would you believe I'm shy, every day I strive to break free?
I'm an artist of little renown, painting watercolour flowers,
landscapes, I'll sometimes be found.

In earlier days golfing was my passion, I'm a proud ex-Lady Captain,
winner of trophies and cups.
I'm a poet, so they tell me, recovering from shock.
Also, a fan of music, avid reader of libraries of books.
I'm a seasoned traveller, lover of exotic destinations, both at
home and away.
I wonder where have all the years gone?
I'm supposed to be living in my golden age, instead sadly,
I'll only remember you, and your name for two minutes.
I feel frumpy, disconcerted, not ready for the aches and pains
of old age.
Still, I'm at peace, feeling content to be me.

Carolyne Crawford

ALL SHADES OF ME

Am I blue or am I black?
Only when I wear a mudpack.
Am I green or am I white?
Only if I stand in candlelight.
Am I red or am I grey?
Neither until I pass away.
Am I purple or am I orange?
Not unless I am a blancmange.
Am I brown or am I rose?
All I can say is, 'heaven knows.'

Ann Brady

Midsummer

A MIDSUMMER'S FAIRY-TALE

Once upon a Midsummer's eve, deep in the dark, spooky forest,
not a whisper of a breeze, or a small dormouse stirred;
Only the distant hooting of a wise old owl could be heard.
In a small clearing, silvery moonbeams dance through the air,
on the shortest, most auspicious night of the year.
By the light of the mystical moon, on a grassy knoll covered in fairy rings,
powerful magic begins.
A special gathering is to be held for all fairies, pixies and elves.
From near and far, on gossamer wings, tiny folk appear,
all smartly dressed in their best;
Wearing pretty garlands of flowers, daisies, buttercups, bluebells,
wild roses, dainty, lacy, green ferns to impress.
On cue, glowing fireflies take off into the night, performing their spectacular aerial
flight.
A fanfare of horns heralds the arrival of their Imperial Fairy King, and his ethereal, shimmering Queen.

Cheers of happiness and joy, complete our magical scene.
They feast on scrumptious forest fruits;
drink nectar served in acorn cups, flown in by gracious, busy, bee recruits.
The whole night long, under sparkling stars, they prance, dance to the music of the fabulous, famous beetle band.
After a wonderful night, exhausted, hardly able to stand,
the Fairy King raises his magical wand;
In a blinding flash, all revellers disappear into the first golden rays of the new day.
Dawn breaks, early birds sweetly sing, baby rabbits awake, anxious to play.
On the forest's ferny floor only, piles of broken acorns remain,
until next year, when fairy magic will begin all over again.

Carolyne Crawford

Midsummer's eve at Stonehenge, people amass,
to view the ancient glories of this wonder.
From far and wide, to the Wiltshire
countryside,
People and converging lay lines meet.
At sunrise, the old, young, Ancients, and
Druids, stand together, their feet anchored in
the deep, lush grass, waiting in reverence for
the sky to clear, the rays
of sunlight to shine on the Heel Stone,
into the heart of the Henge circle, where, full of
mystical overtones, the sun's brightness falls.
For many thousands of years, in this same place
the Midsummer Solstice has been welcomed.

                              Lis McDermott

Severed Heart

SEVERED HEART

If you wake and smile at me
In your eyes your love I'll see
But if you cannot look into my eyes
I'll know our love has finally died
And so, my heart will no longer feel
For severed now my blood will congeal

                    Ann Brady

In the stillness of night
when the darkness is blackest,
and shadows appear indistinct,
You lie alone, full of incredulity,
Unable to grasp your solitude is at his behest,
Yet, alone you lie, struggling with the cruelty
that has befallen you.
You are no longer loved,
The sound of your feet running
to greet him, forgotten -
lost in the immense, gaping silence.
Now, your body, once awoken by his touch, can
no longer breathe.
Each breath allows your dying soul to seep
from your severed heart,
barely beating like a tragic song bird,
who has mislaid her song…
You pray for night to continue
longer, darker, hypnotically silent,
allowing you to sleep forever.

Lis McDermott

SEVERED HEARTS

What happens to hearts when loving feelings cease?
When unbelief besets your mind and all you crave is peace.
Why don't people want you, who have loved you once before?
Severed, sorrowful hearts can they ever be restored?

No amount of solace will dull a painful, broken heart;
Still desolate feelings, after lover's part,
Or stop yearnings to turn back time,
To earlier, happier days, sublime.
False hope is a new best friend,
Truth be told, love has reached the bitter end.
Life continues on in its own inevitable, chaotic way,
It can be a daunting task, to find true love today.
No one needs the heartache, or the absence of love's lack;
Severed hearts can only be healed when you accept lost lovers back.

Carolyne Crawford

Misguided Words

CRISIS

I have walked all day with poems in my head –
metaphors bumping into each other,
alliterations a party of three,
errant rhyme schemes erring
on the side of carefree.

Yet when I sit down to write,
pen poetically poised above paper,
holding my breath -
as if the poem will hear my human exhales
tumbling out of my lungs in waves
and decide to walk away.

I can no longer remember
what inspired me
to unpack my writing utensils
from their pristine cages.
I stand, peering into the depths of the forest,
a tourist peeping into windows
to get a taste of local life,
as time hangs suspended in a limbo.

Finally, I sit back, satisfied,
without having written a single line.

Greeshma Rajeev

MISGUIDED WORDS

The opinions of the world will bring you down,
Don't be swayed, quietly walk away.
Misguided words will make you frown.

No matter how wise the words may sound,
Take heed, fools are easily led astray.
The opinions of the world will bring you down.

Ultimately, dire circumstances may rebound.
Seek out wise advice, without delay.
Misguided words will make you frown.

Keep calm, or your problems will compound.
Impulsive decision-making is not okay.
The opinions of the world will bring you down.

Search your heart to seek a common ground.
Take time to rationalise your thoughts today.
Misguided words will make you frown.

Right or wrong, free-will abounds.
Personal moral codes do not betray.
The opinions of the world will bring you down,
Misguided words will make you frown.

    Carolyne Crawford

Your words were so cruel and thoughtless,
Knowing how she felt about her weight,
It's not surprising she suffered from stress.
The names you called her, so inappropriate.

Then giving her false hope, of what she might achieve,
By your words you proved you agreed, she was flawed
Your advice underlined everything she herself, believed;
As a friend, you ended up being a complete fraud.

Comments that in hindsight can be seen as imprudent,
Were spoken without malice, yet their understanding mistaken
Her sadness deeply held, her death ended the punishment.

                        Lis McDermott

Overheard Conversations

IMAGINARY LINE

An explanation of the misunderstood, Offside rule,
Overheard, between two middle aged friends,
who'd obviously had to watch the Euro's at
weekends;
The husband of one's, comments had made her feel a
fool.

She had focussed hard to gain an understanding,
and now was waxing lyrical, her explanation,
expanding.

Becoming impatient with her friend, using
condiments
laid out across the table; cups, sachets of sugar, salt,
She explained where players would fall foul, be at
fault,
if they crossed the imaginary line, when the offside
rule presents.

I pondered, if only there was a visible, imaginary line
in life, it might even help tragic events turn out fine.

Crossing that line, mid argument or discussion,
if it were visible to the eye, you'd recognise
when you are about to say something hurtful, unwise;
If tangible, you could ward-off any repercussion.

Visible, rather than imaginary lines would be a god-send,
Maybe bringing many global arguments to an end!

Lis McDermott

MY CUP OF TEA!

"She's a liar," stated the woman, "of that there is no doubt.
Look at all the horrible, nasty things she did spout.
Our lady, she would never have been so cruel or unkind.
She should have kicked that woman up her fat behind."

"You're wrong, you know," the other woman declared.
"That woman is an angel, about which no-one really cared.
She was filled with fears of suicide that pulled her down.
Even making our poor, sweet handsome Prince to frown."

"Oh, don't be so daft, the blooming pair of you."
Can you not see the stupidity of what you say and view?
The woman has been caught out, that is a fact.
So, stop this bickering and stupid act.

And don't forget she was caught out in most of what she said,
We all know it's because she's obviously wrong in the head.
So, please stop your arguing and agree to disagree,
Cause' I'm feeling hungry and I want my cup of tea."

                    Ann Brady

SALAMANDER

Yesterday, I learnt that
giving a salamander all your love,
and attention, and care,
can quite often kill it -
naïve intentions morph
into murderous instincts.

This morsel of truth
plants itself in my brain.
I grab my keys,
head out the door again,
and this time, I decide to let go
of all that I cannot force
into existence.

I am tense, but relieved,
both the soldier and the bereaved.

               Greeshma Rajeev

IT'S COCKTAIL TIME

The bar's open, Happy Hour is cocktail time!
Sip a favourite cocktail, or try a new taste bud sensation,
With friends, at a posh event, any place or time.
Feeling good, bad, happy or sad, a cocktail or two will get you through.
Try a divine *Pina Colada* on a Caribbean beach in the sun.
Have fun drinking a *Tequila Sunrise, Margarita* at parties.
Maybe your thing is a *Singapore Sling,* or downing a fruity *Ding-a-ling.*
Not to mention an *Alabama Slammer, Sex on a beach,*
Cosmopolitan, or yummy *Death in the afternoon.*
All shaken, not stirred by a sexy bartender with the dexterity, charm of a young Tom Cruise.
Cheers to a happy, cocktail-delicious, good time.

                      Carolyne Crawford

Sun Kissed

SUN KISSED

Sometimes when it rains
the clouds are on the inside.
You step out, breathe in
the sunshine, let it all go.
Much to your surprise,
when you come back home, you find
the sunshine has followed you.

>   Greeshma Rajeev

MY SUN KISSED FRIEND

Digging deep beneath the ground, I'll place a tiny seed,
With care, sun and lots of water, I'll give you all you need.
I know to put you in a well-drained place, so you can live your life.
With care and love, I'm sure that you, will grow to quite a height

I've prepared the soil by digging deep, at least I'm down two feet.
Making sure there's lots of room, for you'll grow bigger than the wheat.
And so the days will pass us by, and up and up you'll grow
Until, eventually one bright day you'll put on quite a show.

And as I'll look into your face, you know that I will smile.
What a sunny look you'll have, standing proudly tall with style.
Gently in the breeze you'll move, swinging slowly here and there,
as your beautiful sun-kissed head, floats majestically in the air.

                                        Ann Brady

BY THE OCEAN

On the beach sit two sun-kissed people,
People lost in their emotions,
Emotionally drawn to the ocean,
Oceans apart in love and devotion.

Lost in nostalgic memories of the past,
Past-times of blissful happiness, joyous love,
Loving, dreaming of a future together,
Together as one, in perfect harmony.

Mutual distrust, suspicious thoughts arise,
Rising, mingling with dark shadows in their mind,
Mindful of the inevitable sorrow of heartbreak,
Heartbreakingly, they agree a tender kiss, goodbye.

                                Carolyne Crawford

SUN KISSED

Dappled skin, freckled and sweet,
With the fragrance of ripe peaches,
She moved in a way that was easy, hips swaying
As though dancing to an invisible, lilting song.
He waited, watching her, as her lithe legs,
pointed toes, picked out a pathway
through the seashells, strewn on the sand.
Aware of the envious eyes, hidden beneath brims
of hats, beneath parasols, partners scowling,
wives comparing their shapes to hers.
Unaware, arriving in front of his lounger,
she stooped, and her luscious lips, met his,
She was his sun kissed lover; she, his entire life,
Born of the sun, his beautiful, younger wife.

                        Lis McDermott

Childhood Memories
Prose poem

CHILDHOOD MEMORIES

I'll always treasure the magical days of childhood with my twin, my identical partner in crime. Life was exciting, hilariously funny, sometimes annoying. I remember the frustration of being asked by all comers, "Gosh, you look alike, are you twins?"
Oh, how I remember the delightful feeling of power, when I realised Mum had a problem telling us apart. I remember I was never lonely, with my twin by my side.
When small, mischief and pranks were the order of the day. There were times, I recall when sibling rivalry kicked in, tempers rose, all hell broke loose, later we kissed and made-up. I remember when we were four, she helped me climb up onto
 a chair, to reach Dad's treasured pendulum clock. The clock with the cute, tiny door in the back. Inside the pendulum mesmerisingly, swung to and fro. I remember things were going okay, until …. let me think, was it her, or me who decided to smash it to bits? I do remember Dad's unearthly scream, when later he discovered the dreadful, broken mess on the floor. Painfully, I remember we were sentenced to bed, with no sweets for a week. Not one of our finest moments, not a great day at all.

                              Carolyne Crawford

AMOOMA

My grandmother will always know me as a five-year-old. I ache thinking of her, perched among the clouds, rummaging through nursery schools for my face. I look nothing like that little girl now, but she didn't stick around long enough to find that out.
I moved cities, changed identities, let go of my crazy theories that love, and only love, was going to save me. I saved myself. She would have been proud.
The woman who took the blame when I spilt watercolour water onto my grandfather's precious veranda. The woman who descended steps, one at a time, turned to the left. I never asked her why, but each time I find myself on top of a steep slope, I turn to the left, descend, one foot at a time, hoping that my grandmother looks away from the playground and catches my eye.

                              Greeshma Rajeev

TIPPY, TIPPY TOES

Point your toes; one, two, three. Turn around and come back to me. Lift your leg, keeping it spread out straight, remembering to balance with your weight. Put your foot down upon the ground making sure you don't make a sound. Now you must try with the other leg, keeping this one as straight as a peg.

With both feet back down on the floor balance your body and centre your core. Slowly lift the hem of your skirt, holding it out to look like a creamy dessert of tasty strawberries and fluffy cream, before you close your eyes and start to dream.

Up, up on your toes you start to elevate. Do not be frightened, do not hesitate. For you are going to achieve your dream, as in your imagination you create a theme. For now, you have become the one and only Katarina. That wonderful, famous, beautiful dancing ballerina.

Ann Brady

I WAS A DADDY'S GIRL

I was a daddy's' girl. When small, he would stand me on his feet and waltz around the room. At bath-time, we sang songs together, as he dried me in a large towel, his voice surrounding me in comfort.
I was a daddy's girl. On holidays my hand clasped tightly in his, we'd stand at the water's edge, as we dipped our feet into the cold sea. He carved boats in the sand, even created a seat, where I imagined rowing on the waters of the sea; long before my adult fears stopped me from ever swimming in the ocean.
I was a daddy' girl. At weekends we'd win the argument to watch cowboy films on TV, which Mum didn't enjoy. Even now, I love them, black and white films with long dead actors riding in to the sunset.
I was a daddy's girl. At fifty-six, a week before my nineteenth birthday, he died too young, locking him into my heart forever, frozen in time.
I was a daddy's girl. Even after his death, I'd see him, tall, bald headed, walking down the street towards, me, or walking away in the crowd with his individual gait and my heart would beat faster with counterfeit hope.

Lis McDermott

Story poem about someone with an usual name.

SIR GARSTANG THE GORGEOUS

Sir Garstang the Gorgeous was a knight of old,
From a tender age he was trained to be
gallant and bold.
On his trusty steed, sword and shield in hand,
For God, king and country, he rode through the land.

Challenges aplenty he suffered in life;
For his dashing good looks incited jealousy and
strife.
The sight of him clad in shining armour, dazzling
chain-mail,
caused many a lady to swoon, his charisma never did
fail.

He was a legend at tournaments, scarcely suffered
defeat.
Ladies bestowed 'favours' by the score, sharing
smiles so sweet,
in the hope of his undying attentions, passionate love
and romance.
Scorned by his fellow knights, he led them a pretty
dance.

His favourite quest, was to rescue poor damsels in distress;
Sword drawn, bow at the ready to shoot and impress.
As Queen's champion his attentions were considered bold,
Until the King discovered he was being cuckold.

For his treachery he was exiled to the Holy land
To fight and conquer the infidel foe, a cruel reprimand.
Much to the ladies' great sorrow and woe, that he was banished.
Further reports of Garstang the Gorgeous have long since vanished,
Remembered only in rhyme, he is lost in the dark, swirling mists of time.

         Carolyne Crawford

ALOISIUS SPARROWHAWK

He was incredibly tiny as a child, was Aloisius Sparrowhawk
And generally, all that could be heard from his mouth, was a squawk.
Throughout his schooling one would expect him to have been bullied,
Yet not once did he have a bloodied nose, nor was his name sullied -

by his class-mates, or those he met; no cases of mudslinging or vilification
seemed to occur during his time at nursery, or school or even the whole duration.
After years of remaining silent, yet somehow, still in control, Aloisius Sparrowhawk
'out of the blue', at the age of sixteen and three quarters, began to talk.

A voice completely unexpected, assertive, one of power and command,
No small talk or waffle, but with each word you were held in the palm of his hand.

From an inauspicious start of a squeak, Aloisius had
found his life journey to walk,
earning millions, talking to his global radio audience,
in the guise of Nighthawk.

                        Lis McDermott

POETS INFORMATION, AND THE PAGES THEIR POETRY APPEARS.

Ann Brady is a published author, mentor, publisher and part-time poet. The latter she does for fun. Ann is based in Cardiff and has published a range of books, including an award-winning historical novel, a children's picture book series, plus a variety of other genres. She mentors' writers of all ages and has published a number of books written by younger writers.

www.ann-brady.co.uk
www.mentoringwriters.co.uk

Poetry Pages: 12, 39, 48, 52, 62, 78, 83, 92, 103, 109, 110, 114, 120, 128, 132, 140, 146, 152, 194, 200, 210, 217, 224

Carolyne Crawford was born (b. 1950) and raised in Middlesbrough, in the North-East of England. She now lives in Wiltshire with her husband, two daughters and six grandsons.

After a successful secretarial career in banking, law and working for the Personnel Department of a famous French Perfumery House she retired early, took some golf lessons and became a golfing addict. She is a nature lover, especially passionate about her garden, plays Bridge, dabbles in watercolour painting, and is an avid reader of all genre.

With no previous writing experience, she wrote her first poem 7 years ago, taking inspiration from her Christian faith. She feels blessed to have joined Lis' Poetry Group of talented poets, and hopes to continue writing, reading, enjoying poetry
for the foreseeable future

Poetry Pages: 8, 15,20, 27, 34, 38, 44, 51, 57, 66, 68, 72, 76, 79, 84, 86, 93, 96, 104, 108, 116, 126, 130, 133, 136, 145, 150, 156, 161, 165, 170, 178, 184, 192, 196, 202, 205, 213, 218, 222, 228

Lis McDermott who started the poetry group, is a published author and poet. She is based in Wiltshire, where she lives with her husband. After a successful career in music education, where she worked for 34 years, Lis started her own photography business where she worked for 12 years. She began writing seriously in 2017 and now works as a writing mentor. Lis has now published a range of books, including short stories, an autobiography, four poetry books and her first novel, is due to be published in the new year.

www.LisMcDermottAuthor.co.uk

Poetry Pages: 7, 16, 18, 32, 40, 46, 50, 58, 64, 70, 73, 80, 82, 90, 98, 105, 112, 115, 124, 129, 134, 137, 147, 153, 157, 160, 167, 173, 180, 183, 187, 190, 198, 201, 206, 208, 219, 225, 230

Greeshma Rajeev grew up in different cities across Asia but she belongs to India and now lives in London. She used to work in marketing and recruitment but quit her job a few months ago to teach English. She hopes to be able to inspire young people to love literature someday. Last year, during lockdown, Greeshma started writing poetry. She found that the moments of silence that led to her poems helped her cope with stress and be brave. Greeshma keeps writing in an attempt to make sense of the world inside and outside of her.

Recently her poetry has been published in the *Verse of Silence June 2021 Edition.* Alongside training to be a teacher, she is also working towards publishing her poetry collection. Watch this space.

Poetry Pages: 6, 13, 22, 28, 35, 42, 60, 88, 97, 122, 138, 154, 157, 166, 177, 182, 186, 204, 212, 216, 223

Naman Kumar is a Software Engineering professional and a poet by heart, based in the United Kingdom. Born and brought up in India, Naman completed his studies in India and moved to the UK for work. Poetry is a hobby but more a friend for Naman that accompanies him in his highs and strengthens him in his lows. Naman is working on getting his first anthology "The Colourless Water" to be published soon.

Poetry Pages: 10, 14, 23, 26, 33, 56, 94, 99, 102, 144, 156, 162, 164, 172, 176, 186

If you are interested in joining **Lis' Poetry Place**, please contact her on:

Lis@lismcdermottauthor.co.uk

Read more about the group at:

https://lismcdermottauthor.co.uk/poetry-place.html

www.ingramcontent.com/pod-product-compliance
Lightning Source LLC
Chambersburg PA
CBHW022112040426
42450CB00006B/668